UPPER INTERMEDIATE LEVEL
CLASSICAL PIANO MASTERS
13 PIECES BY 8 COMPOSERS

ISBN 978-1-5400-8402-6

Visit Hal Leonard Online at
www.halleonard.com

Contact us:
Hal Leonard
7777 West Bluemound Road
Milwaukee, WI 53213
Email: info@halleonard.com

In Europe, contact:
Hal Leonard Europe Limited
42 Wigmore Street
Marylebone, London, W1U 2RN
Email: info@halleonardeurope.com

In Australia, contact:
Hal Leonard Australia Pty. Ltd.
4 Lentara Court
Cheltenham, Victoria, 3192 Australia
Email: info@halleonard.com.au

CONTENTS

NOCTURNE IN F MINOR
Op. 55, No. 1

FRÉDÉRIC CHOPIN
1810–1849

POLONAISE IN A MAJOR
"Militaire"
Op. 40, No. 1

FRÉDÉRIC CHOPIN
1810–1849

Allegro con brio

WALTZ IN D-FLAT MAJOR

"Minute"
Op. 64, No. 1

FRÉDÉRIC CHOPIN
1810–1849

16

WALTZ IN C-SHARP MINOR
Op. 64, No. 2

FRÉDÉRIC CHOPIN
1810–1849

WALTZ IN A-FLAT MAJOR
Op. 39, No. 15

JOHANNES BRAHMS
1833–1897

THE CASCADES
A Rag

SCOTT JOPLIN
1868–1919

Tempo di Marcia

LIEBESTRAUM NO. 3
from THREE LIEBESTRÄUME

FRANZ LISZT
1811–1886

SPRING SONG
from SONGS WITHOUT WORDS, Op. 62, No. 6

FELIX MENDELSSOHN
1809–1847

Allegretto grazioso

12 VARIATIONS
On AH! VOUS DIRAI-JE, MAMAN
K. 265

WOLFGANG AMADEUS MOZART
1756–1791

Theme

VAR. I

RONDO ALLA TURCA
from SONATA IN A MAJOR, K. 331

WOLFGANG AMADEUS MOZART
1756–1791

JUNE (BARCAROLLE)
from THE SEASONS, Op. 37b

PYOTR IL'YICH TCHAIKOVSKY
1840–1893

Andante cantabile

PRELUDE IN G MINOR
Op. 23, No. 5

SERGEI RACHMANINOFF
1873–1943

Alla marcia (♩ = 108)

Poco meno mosso

PRELUDE IN C-SHARP MINOR
Op. 3, No. 2

SERGEI RACHMANINOFF
1873–1943

Agitato

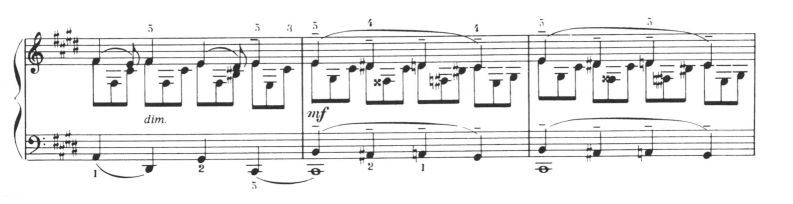

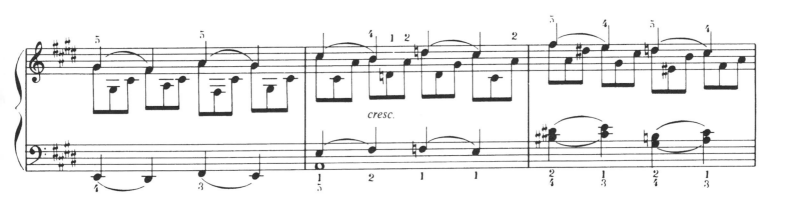

61

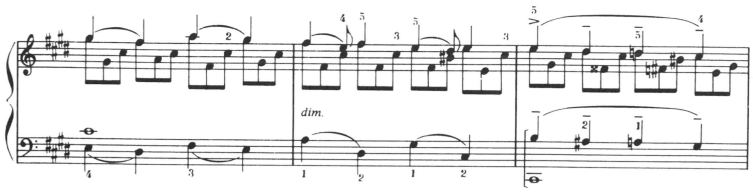

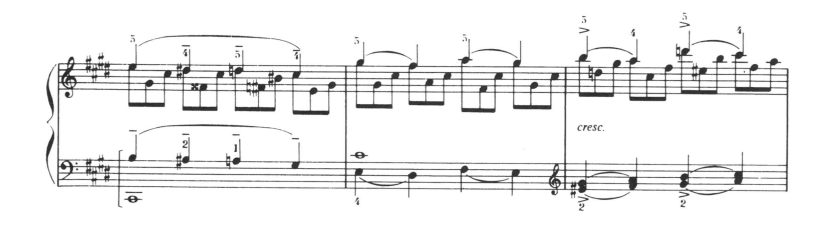

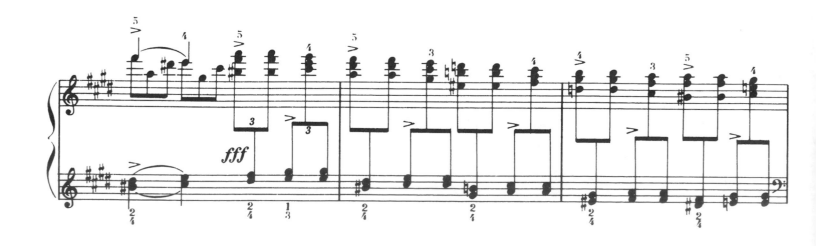

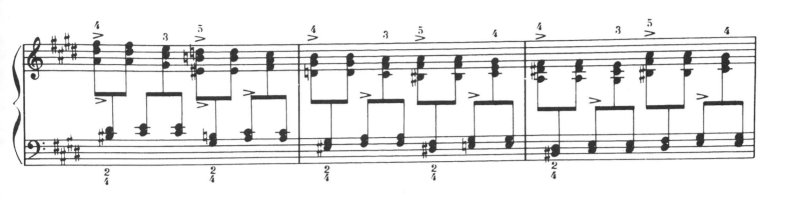

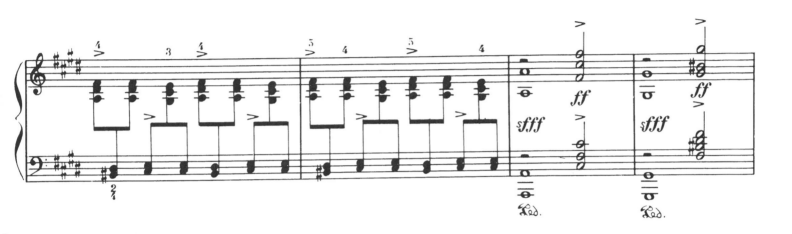

Tempo I°